André Claude BAYOMOCK LINWA
Essetchi Desnos YECHI

Social networking and thematic QoS databases: the foundation of a smart city

André Claude BAYOMOCK LINWA
Essetchi Desnos YECHI

Social networking and thematic QoS databases: the foundation of a smart city

ScienciaScripts

Imprint

Cover image: www.ingimage.com

This book is a translation from the original published under ISBN 978-620-6-72518-3.

Publisher:
Sciencia Scripts
is a trademark of
Dodo Books Indian Ocean Ltd. and OmniScriptum S.R.L publishing group

120 High Road, East Finchley, London, N2 9ED, United Kingdom
Str. Armeneasca 28/1, office 1, Chisinau MD-2012, Republic of Moldova, Europe
Printed at: see last page
ISBN: 978-620-8-26764-3

SOCIAL NETWORK AND THEMATIC QOS DATABASE: THE FOUNDATION OF A SMART CITY

DR. BAYOMOCK LINWA ANDRE CLAUDE
DEPARTMENT OF COMPUTER SCIENCE,
INTERNATIONAL UNIVERSITY OF GRAND-BASSAM
BAYOMOCK.A@IUGB.EDU.CI

MR. YECHI ESSETCHI DESNOS
MASTER 2 BDGL, UFR DEPARTMENT
MATHEMATICS AND COMPUTER SCIENCE, UNIVERSITE FELIX HOUPHOUËT BOIGNY
YECHIDESNOS@HOTMAIL.COM

TABLE OF CONTENTS

ABSTRACT

The 21st century has seen the rise of diverse information sources, from traditional media to private and citizen media. While traditional media may be influenced externally and not always reflect facts accurately, citizen media allows for free expression where individuals can share their observations and experiences. These citizen sources provide valuable insights into urban life, contributing data on education, safety, traffic incidents, healthcare, cultural and sports activities, and infrastructure conditions. Properly collected and analysed, this information can help urban administrations enhance service quality and proactively address community needs. This article explores methods for cleaning, transforming, structuring, and storing these citizen data streams for effective querying. In collaboration with city administrators and residents, we will identify key quality of service (QoS) parameters and develop a coordinated protocol to increase the smart city capabilities. The goal is to ensure frequent data updates, within 24 hours or less, to maintain relevance and responsiveness. The document is structured as follows: introduction, research motivations, literature review on QoS in smart cities, problem statement and challenges, solution approach, next steps, and a conclusion summarizing key contributions and future work directions.

Keywords: Smart city, Quality of service (QoS), Social networks, Data models, Economic intelligence, Citizen data collection, Coordination protocol.

1 INTRODUCTION

The smart city is a set of concepts and services that many cities are using to offer better services to their residents. These services require the implementation and deployment of technologies. The foundation of information technologies is based on cabling and interconnection of networks of neighbourhoods, roads and objects, making it possible to provide the city with virtually real-time information following an event or to provide city services through a one-stop shop. While the concept and services are within the financial and technological reach of northern countries, the same cannot be said of southern countries. And yet the concept is attractive, but the deployment of the solution with the standard approach based on a network connection of objects, sensors or sensors is not within the reach of the countries of the South. In this project, we are proposing an alternative solution that uses the connectivity of young people in social networks to feed and maintain an information system collecting data linked to an event. The solution consists of documenting events by theme, then defining a protocol for collecting the data, allowing residents to give their opinions on an event, to consult the events, and to propose solutions for improving the performance of the subject in question. Residents, thanks to their proximity and daily experience, can provide valuable data on various aspects such as education, safety, traffic incidents, healthcare, cultural and sporting activities, and the state of infrastructures. This information, if properly collected and analysed, can help urban administrations to improve the quality of services offered to citizens and to respond proactively to community needs and concerns. In collaboration with the city's administrators (mayor or councillors) and residents, we will identify the essential quality of service (QoS) parameters and develop a suitable data model for exploiting this information. The aim is to collect real information about what is happening in the city so that the city, through its technological platform can inform its population and take their opinions on board. In short, this process will guarantee the relevance and responsiveness of information for the intelligent city. This document is structured as follows: after the introduction, we present the motivations for this research. Next, we will review the existing literature on quality of service in smart cities. We will then describe the problem to be solved and the associated challenges. We will then outline our solution approach and discuss the next steps. Finally, we will conclude by summarising the main contributions of our study and suggesting avenues for future work.

2 MOTIVATIONS

The way cities are evolving today is intimately linked to information technology. These technologies have not only transformed the way we live, but are also shaping our future. There is therefore a genuine correlation between humans and technology, a metaphor borrowed from biology (Bender, De Haan, & Bennett, 1995; Brangier, 2002, 2003; Griffith, 2006; De Rosnay, 2000). This perspective demonstrates the need to go beyond the traditional opposition between human and technology (Simondon, 1958), particularly because "anthropology has empirically established that anthropogenesis is empirically technogenesis" (Stiegler, 1989). In other words, technological advances are not simply external tools used by humanity, but form an integral part of its evolutionary process and the way it transforms itself as a species.

Aware of this co-evolution and concerned about the well-being it can bring, a number of studies have shown that technology greatly facilitates people's daily lives. With this in mind, our mission is to give people and urban administrators real-time knowledge of what's happening in their city. The aim of the project is to optimise decision-making by basing it on concrete facts and providing classified information for easy, structured reading of events.

To achieve this, we have decided to actively involve the city's residents in the information-gathering process. These citizens will use an appropriate social network and a clear protocol to inform the smart city's information system. Once collected, this information is processed and made available to residents, administrators and all stakeholders, according to their specific needs.

This approach is our main motivation. It is important to note that, following our literature review, we did not find any subject that corresponded perfectly to our motivations and objectives as set out above.

3 REVIEW OF LITERATURE

Smart cities are made up of multiple intelligence segments: infrastructure, healthcare, buildings, transport and education. These segments of intelligence form the foundation of smart cities that perform well in delivering services (Mohanty et al., 2016). If the infrastructures were to fail, the very concept of the smart city would be called into question from the point of view of the unavailability of the information flow back to the requesting source. A number of studies have been carried out to prevent this from happening, and to ensure that the intelligent city can continue to offer people a high quality of life.

3.1.1 Network Technologies in Smart Cities

The study by AlZoman and Alenazi (2020) focuses on a new resilient system for smart city networks using Software-Defined Networking (SDN) networking technology. This technology relies on software controllers or APIs (Application Program Interfaces) to direct network traffic and communicate with the underlying hardware infrastructure. SDN makes it possible to create and control a virtual network or to control a traditional hardware network using software. This increases the quality of service of data transport for critical applications following a degradation in the capacity of the transport link. The proposed new system, called Smart City Resilient System (SCRS), includes modules such as TopoDiscovery, FailureDetection, FastDivRoute, TrafficQoS and RulesGenerator.

3.1.2 Quality of Service (QoS) and User Experience (QoE) management

In a study conducted by Tu (2018), the author provides an overview of the main SC services and their functions, as well as the main ICT technologies supporting the applications. He proposes a QoS/QoE management framework based on data mainly from offline training modules and online management modules. Through this layered approach, the author offers a solution for which manages QoE if a large number of different devices/users/applications are used. This solution associates each layer with a specific QoE domain, and the combination of layers (offline and online) to calculate overall performance is effective for QoE control.

3.1.3 Communication Architectures and Protocols

Lloret et al. (2019) proposed a group-based communication architecture and protocol to connect different service infrastructures in smart cities. The proposed system is scalable and fault-tolerant, making it possible to interconnect sensors and networks in smart cities. With the evolution of information and communication technologies, new sensors are being developed to monitor various aspects in large cities, such as the environment, health and traffic. These sensors need to be integrated into wider networks, which in turn need to be interconnected to improve the efficiency and sustainability of cities.

3.1.4 Safety in Smart Cities

Security and crime prevention are often neglected in smart cities. Laufs et al (2020) conducted an extensive search of the literature and compiled a list of security interventions that fell into three categories: those using new sensors but traditional actuators, those aiming to make old systems intelligent, and those introducing entirely new functions. In addition, Ralko and Kumar highlight the importance of smart cities in the daily lives of residents, controlling aspects such as traffic patterns, security cameras and utilities. The authors discuss the potential risks and consequences of a cyber attack on smart city networks, stressing the importance of implementing security controls, training security professionals and allocating adequate budgets to protect smart city cyber infrastructure.

3.1.5 Research opportunity: Collection and Analysis of Citizen Data

Our study focuses on the importance of structuring, analysing and storing citizen data flows efficiently. The aim is to enable anyone with relevant information on specific topics to use our platform to feed information systems in smart cities and query them intelligently. We plan to formulate a questionnaire for city administrators such as the mayor or councillors, as well as residents, to determine the quality of service (QoS) parameters that they would like to be informed about by the inhabitants of a particular part of the city. We will then propose a suitable data model to exploit the information collected.In sum, our literature review shows that there is an abundance of research on the technologies and systems that support smart cities. However, there is a pressing need for integrated solutions that not only interconnect various segments of urban intelligence but also actively involve citizens in the process of collecting and using data. By targeting the identified gaps, our study aims to develop robust methods for harnessing citizen data to improve quality of life and stimulate economic growth in smart cities.

4 PROBLEMS AND CHALLENGES

The smart city concept requires a vast amount of information from a variety of sources. It is crucial to note that the lifespan of information in a smart city is often short. Information sources, whether private or public, are not always on hand to cover and report on events in the city in real time. The problem of road traffic exacerbates the situation in some areas, where it can be extremely difficult for telecoms players to move efficiently from point A to point B in order to collect and disseminate information about a specific event. In addition, cumbersome administrative processes are also a major challenge, because even if the information is available, it often has to be validated by the administrative authorities before it can be made accessible to citizens within a reasonable timeframe. In addition, smart city network infrastructures vary considerably across the world. For example, regions such as South Asia often benefit from richer network connectivity and a high number of Internet users, 1,426.39 million as indicated by Statista statistics in 2023 (Number of Internet users in the world by region 2023, n.d.) (see Figure 1).

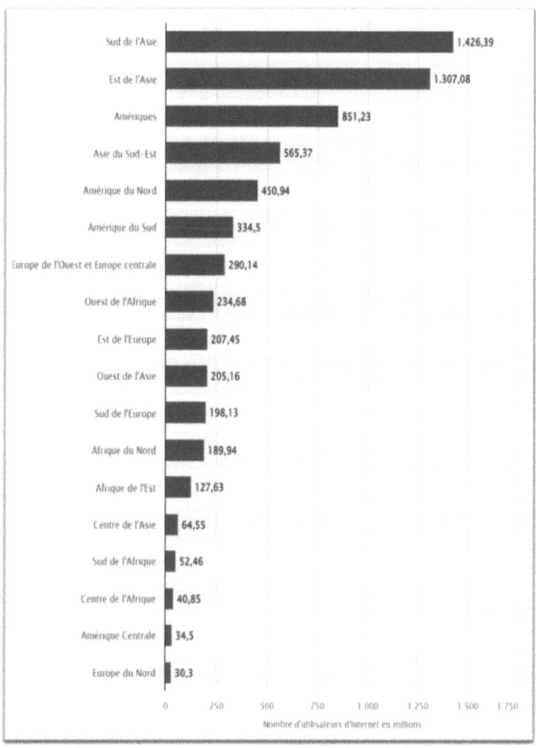

Figure 1: Number of Internet users in the world in 2023, by region (in millions)

Smart cities therefore require extensive interconnection covering various networks such as roads, transport networks, electricity, water and gas distribution, as well as the interconnection of homes. It is also crucial to consider the interconnection of educational establishments such as schools and universities, enabling improved monitoring and management of students. This holistic approach to interconnection helps to improve operational efficiency and resource management in modern urban environments.

5 SOLUTION APPROACH

An intelligent city is one that serves its residents and delivers quality services through information technologies that meet their needs. Our solution is to take into account :

✓ Providing the population with access to information technologies (IT) and using residents' IT skills to make the city intelligent

✓ Organise data collection by structuring the city's intelligence by theme

✓ Analysing the data collected

✓ Define a protocol for deploying thematic intelligence to improve the quality of information offered to residents and support administrators in achieving the objectives set.

✓ Create a suitable data model

✓ Implementing the solution

5.1 Means of public access to IT and use of acquired

Unlike in developed countries, where the INTERNET is deployed in public places and the city has sufficient resources to interconnect several city squares to their city intelligence information databases, in developing countries the Internet is deployed in public places and the city has sufficient resources to interconnect several city squares to their city intelligence information databases. Underdeveloped countries, and sub-Saharan countries in particular, don't have the means to afford it. To solve this problem and enable the city to be close to its residents and offer attractive services at lower cost, we made a simple observation: young people (adolescents and young adults) in sub-Saharan countries spend an average of 8 hours a day connected to social networks. We're building on this experience to offer people the chance to play an active role in generating intelligence in their towns and cities. In this research project, our solution is to develop a private, thematic social network that will inject intelligence into the city and that can be consulted by the city's residents and administrators. It should be noted that our initial idea was to use an existing social network such as Facebook, Instagam or Telegram to generate the intelligent data required, but we found that it was difficult to obtain some of the source code that led to the implementation of these social networks in order to make modifications.

5.2 Organising the collection of intelligent data for the city

The data was collected by approaching the main players in the intelligent city, namely the city's administrators (councillors and city employees) and the city's residents. To this end, a questionnaire was designed and distributed to the administrators, and a web form was set up to allow city residents to express their preferences for the intelligent information to be collected.

5.2.1 The different themes

Table 1: Non-exhaustive list of possible themes

Name of the theme	Description	Importance	Retained for implementation in this project
Education	This theme covers information on the quality of teaching, access to educational resources, school infrastructure and students' academic performance. It also includes data on student satisfaction, parents and teachers.	Education is crucial to people's personal and professional development. Good quality education fosters innovation and long-term economic growth.	YES
Health	This theme encompasses data on the quality of healthcare, access to medical services, hospital infrastructure and patient satisfaction. It may also include public health statistics, such as vaccination rates and local epidemics.	Health is essential to the well-being of individuals and the productivity of society. High-quality health services can improve quality of life and reduce the costs of illness.	NO
Safety	This theme focuses on public safety, including crime rates, safety incidents, law enforcement responsiveness, and public perceptions of safety. It covers also the prevention of	The security is fundamental to ensuring a stable environment conducive to economic and social development. Good security strengthens public confidence and investors.	YES
	Crimes and the management of emergencies.		
Sports	This theme covers sports infrastructure, access to facilities, citizen participation in sports activities, and local sports events. It also includes data on health benefits. associated with physical activity.	Sport is important for promoting a healthy and active lifestyle, strengthening social cohesion and improving quality of life. However, in the context of this project, it is a lower priority than other themes.	NO

Explanation of the Selection

• **Education** and **safety** were chosen for their essential role in the development and well-being of citizens, as well as their direct impact on quality of life and economic development.

• **Health** and **sport**, although very important, have not been included in this specific project, in order to concentrate efforts and resources on areas considered to be priorities in the current context.

5.2.1.1 Forms for "Education" theme

Table 2: Education form sent to city administrators

Questions	Answers expected
What is the current quality of school infrastructure in your town?	Scale from 1 to 5
What are the main challenges facing education?	Free text
What are the current performance indicators used to evaluate the schools?	List of indicators
How would you rate the satisfaction of teachers and staff? educational?	Scale from 1 to 5
What projects or initiatives are underway to improve education in the region?city?	Free text

Table 3: Education web form available to residents of a city

Question	Expected response
Gender	Male/Female/Other
What age group do you belong to?	List of age groups
In which town or city did you live?	Name of town/commune
Please specify the town.	Free text
Profession	List of professions
Does your town of residence provide you with an electronic (virtual) or physical space where you can consult the pass/fail rates of local schools in the various exams?	Yes/No
What is this space?	Free text
Is this school distribution space available at all times?	Yes/No
Does the rate shown take into account how many years have passed?	Number of years
Does your town allow you to use any means (website, physical space, etc.) to rate schools according to their performance?	Yes/No
To your knowledge, how many establishments have a functional infirmary?	Number of establishments
To your knowledge, how many schools have a functional canteen?	Number of establishments
Do schools offer you a space where you can make suggestions for improving school results in your city?	Yes/No
What special programmes or initiatives are in place to support students with special educational needs?	Free text
What are the key indicators you use to measure the quality of the education service provided to pupils?	Free text
Are the establishments located in less noisy areas that are more conducive to learning (away from maquis and bars)?	Yes/No
Have you noticed any fights between pupils in or around schools?	Yes/No
With a view to improving your choice of school for an education in your place of residence, what are your expectations of the town?	Free text

5.2.1.2 Security forms

Table 4: "Safety" form sent to city administrators

Question	Expected response
How would you assess the current public safety situation in your town?	Scale from 1 to 5
What are the main types of crime reported in your city?	List of common crimes
What measures have been put in place to improve safety?	Free text
What are the main challenges facing the police?	Free text
How would you rate the cooperation between the police and the community?	Scale from 1 to 5

Table 5: "Safety" web form available to residents of a city

Question	Expected response
Gender	Male/Female/Other
What age group do you belong to?	List of age groups
In which town/city/neighbourhood did you live?	Name of town/city/neighbourhood
Please specify the town.	Free text
Please specify the area.	Free text
Profession	List of professions
How would you assess the current level of safety in your locality?	Scale from 1 to 5
Which areas of safety do you consider most important to improve? (Tick up to three answers)	List of areas (e.g. crime prevention, road safety, etc.)
Have you ever witnessed or been the victim of crime or security incidents in your city?	Yes/No
Could you briefly describe the incident?	Free text
Have you reported this to the relevant authorities?	Yes/No

How do you rate current communication between local authorities and citizens on safety issues?	Scale from 1 to 5
Would you be in favour of setting up a mobile application to report safety problems in real time?	Yes/No
How do you perceive the level of cooperation between the police and the community in your locality?	Scale from 1 to 5
In your opinion, what are the main causes of insecurity in your locality? (Tick up to three answers)	List of causes (e.g. poverty, unemployment, lack of supervision, etc.)
Would you be prepared to take part in local initiatives to promote safety and strengthen cooperation with the police?	Yes/No
Mention the initiative in a few words.	Free text
Do you have any other suggestions or comments for improving the quality of security services in our city?	Free text

5.2.1.3 Forms for "Health" theme

Table 6: Health form sent to city administrators

Question	Expected response
How would you assess the current public safety situation in your town?	Scale from 1 to 5
What are the main types of crime reported in your city?	List of common crimes
What measures have been put in place to improve safety?	Free text
What are the main challenges facing the police?	Free text
How would you rate cooperation between the police and the community?	Scale from 1 to 5

Table 7: Health web form available to residents of a city

Question	Expected response
Gender	Male/Female/Other
What age group do you belong to?	List of age groups
In which town/city/neighbourhood did you live?	Name from the town/city/neighbourhood
Please specify the town.	Free text
Please specify the area.	Free text
Profession	List of professions
Specify the position	Free text
Do you visit public health establishments?	Yes/No
Why is this?	Free text
How do you find public toilets? reception in the establishments	Scale from 1 to 5
Are you able to pay for medical prescriptions following an illness?	Yes/No
How much can you afford?	Free text (e.g. "0-50%", "51-") 100%", etc.).
Do facilities have in-house pharmacies?	Yes/No
Do schools have in-house laboratories?	Yes/No
What are your expectations of the health establishments in your town?	Free text
Does your home town offer you an electronic (virtual) or physical space where you can give your opinion on the services provided by public health establishments?	Yes/No
What is this space?	Free text
Is this space available at all times?	Yes/No
Does your town allow you to use any means (website, physical space, etc.) to rate schools according to their performance?	Yes/No
Do the establishments offer you a space where you can make suggestions and criticisms to improve the quality of care in your city?	Yes/No

5.2.1.4 Form for theme " Sports

Table 8: "Sports" form sent to city administrators

Question	Expected response
How would you assess the current state of sports facilities in your town?	Scale from 1 to 5
What are the main challenges facing sport?	Free text
What are the current performance indicators used to assess sports facilities?	List indicators
How would you rate user satisfaction with the sports facilities?	Scale from 1 to 5
What projects or initiatives are underway to improve the city's sports infrastructure?	Free text

Table 9: Web form on 'Sports' accessible to residents of a city

Question	Expected response
Gender	Male/Female/Other
What age group do you belong to?	List of age groups
Which town or city do you live in?	Name of town/commune
Please specify the area.	Free text
Profession	List of professions
Specify the position	Free text
Does your home town provide you with an electronic (virtual) or physical space where you can consult the various sports sites and programmes held there?	Yes/No
What is this space? (Give the name.)	Free text
Is this sports broadcasting space available at all times?	Yes/No
How long before events take place is the information generally available?	Free text (e.g. "1 week", "1 month", etc.)

Does your town allow you to use any means (website, physical space, etc.) to rate schools on the organisation and quality of their sports facilities?	Yes/No
Do the establishments offer you a space where you can make suggestions about the type of programmes you would like to take part in in your city?	Yes/No
What special programmes or initiatives have been put in place to enable the population to participate actively in the various sports programmes taking place in the city? (Name them)	Free text
What key indicators do you use to measure the quality of service provided by sports organisations?	List of indicators (e.g. cleanliness, welcome, etc.)
Are the establishments accessible to all? Men, women, disabled ...	Yes/No
Have you noticed any fights between fans in or around sports areas?	Yes/No
Which sport?	Name of sport
What is the most popular sporting event in your city?	Name of event
What suggestions do you have for getting people interested in sport?	Free text

5.3 Analysis of data

5.3.1 Analysis of the data collected on the Education form

5.3.1.1 Location and profession of participants

The data on the education form was collected from 45 people, 29 of them men and 16 women. The table below shows the distribution of respondents by locality and gender.

Table 10: Breakdown of people by locality, occupation and gender

TOWNS/ COMMUNES PROFESSION	Abobo	Adjame	Attecoube	Bingerville	Cocody	Dabakala	Daloa	Danane	Duekoue	Duekoué	Marcory	Saioua	Treichville	Yamoussoukro	Yopougon	Total
Developer	1															1
F	1															1
Student	5	2		2	4		1						1	2	11	28
F		2		2	1		1						1	1	3	11
H	5				3									1	8	17
Nurse											1					1
F											1					1
Engineer					1											1
H					1											1
IT Support				1												1
H				1												1
Teacher			1			1		1			1	1			1	6
F												1				1
H			1			1		1			1				1	5
Technical Assistant										2						2
H										2						2
Radiologist									1							1
H									1							1
Health agent										2						2
F										2						2
Data Manager									1							1
H									1							1
Businessman				1												1
H				1												1
Total	6	2	1	4	5	1	1	1	2	4	2	1	1	2	12	45

There was a high turnout of students: 28 (62%), 11 of whom lived in Yopougon (39%).

5.3.1.2 The gender of the participants

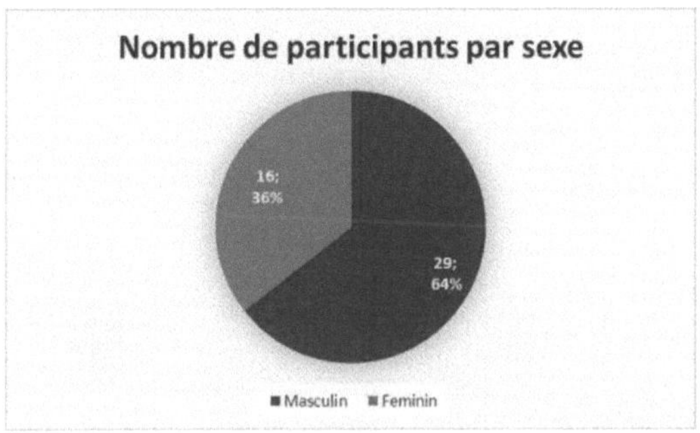

Figure 2: Number of participants by gender

A total of 45 people completed the education questionnaire. The study population was predominantly male, 64% (29/45), compared with 36% (16/45) female.

5.3.1.3 Age range of participants

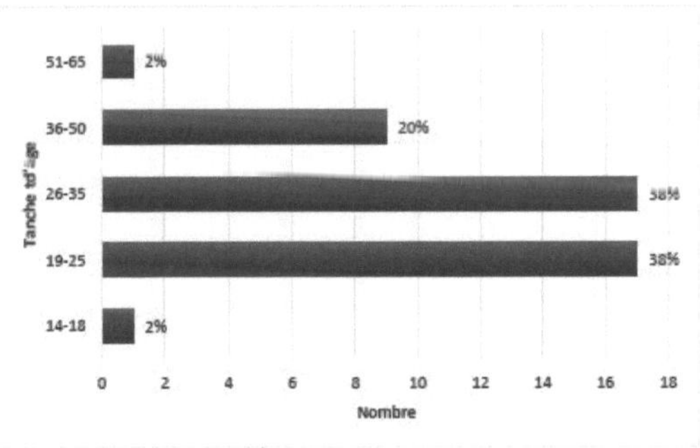

Figure 3: Breakdown by age group

There was a high level of participation from people aged between 19 and 35 for the education questionnaire.

5.3.1.4 Availability of digital space according to participants

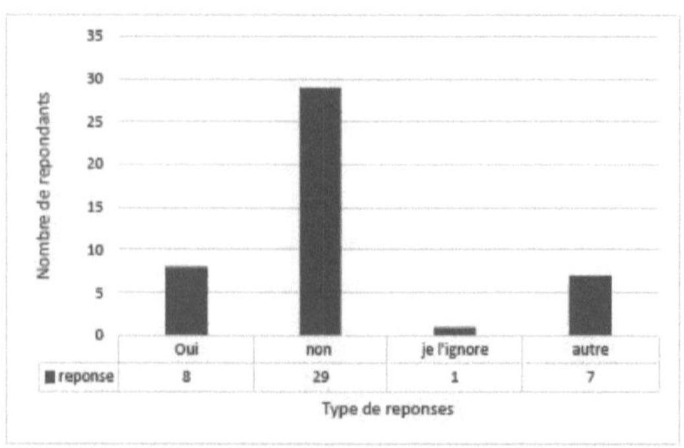

Figure 4: Breakdown of responses on the availability of digital space.

29 people, or 64% of respondents, said that they did not have a digital space available where they could consult information on what was being done in education in their locality. However, the following table shows the spaces available.

Table 11: Type of space available

Number of people	Digital space	Physical space
2	Facebook	
1	Google	
1	www.mena.org	
1		DRENNA
3		School

5.3.2 Analysis of data collected (Security)

5.3.2.1 Location and profession of participants

The data was collected from 39 people, 26 men and 13 women. The table below shows the breakdown of respondents by locality and gender.

Table 12: Breakdown of people by locality, occupation and gender

Town/commune Profession	Abobo	Adjame	Bingerville	Cocody	Daloa	Duekoue	Ferkessedougou	Kong	Koumassi	Mbengue	Treichville	Yamoussoukro	Yopougon	Total
Health agent						1								1
H						1								1
Operations officer/private security		1												1
H		1												1
Technical Assistant						1								1
H						1								1
executive assistant													1	1
F													1	1
Student	2	1	2	1				1	1		2	1	4	15
F		1	1					1	1		2		2	8
H	2		1	1								1	2	7
IT		1												1
H		1												1
ENGINEER				2										2
H				2										2
Network and Security Engineer											1			1
H											1			1
teacher							1							1
F							1							1
Professor													1	1
H													1	1
Trainee									1					1
H									1					1
IT Support			1											1
H			1											1
Treasurer				1										1
H				1										1
Student	1	1	1	1	1					1			5	11
F		1	1		1									3
H	1			1						1			5	8
Total	3	4	4	5	1	2	1	1	2	1	3	1	11	39

There was a high turnout of 15 students, or 39%.

5.3.2.2 The gender of the participants

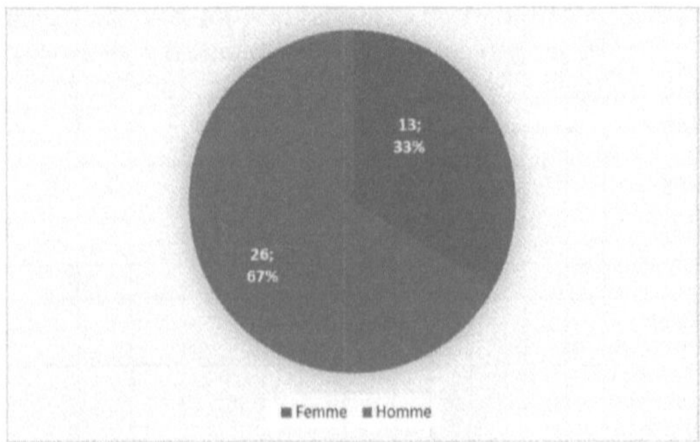

Figure 5: Number of participants by gender

5.3.2.3 Age range of participants

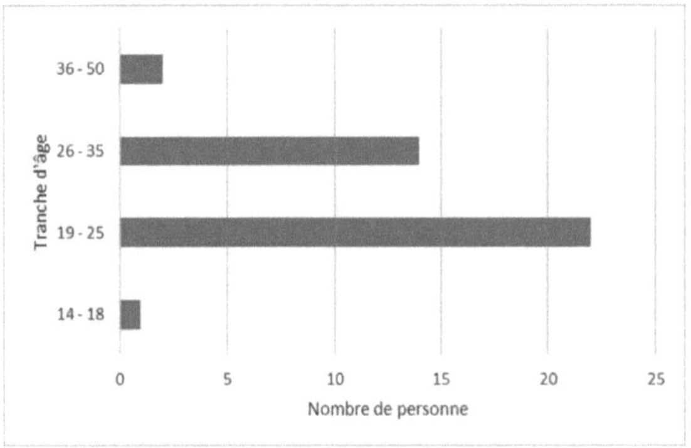

Figure 6: Breakdown by age group

There was a high level of participation in the safety questionnaire by people aged between 19 and 35.

5.3.2.4 Satisfaction index

Index of satisfaction	Workforce	Percentage
Unsatisfactory	10	26%
Neutral	10	26%
Satisfactory	13	33%
Very unsatisfactory	4	10%
Very satisfactory	2	5%
Total	39	100%

Table 13: Breakdown of responses by satisfaction index

Of the 39 respondents to the question "How do you currently rate the level of safety in your locality?" the majority answered that they were **satisfied** with 13 responses, followed by an equal number of responses in **the "Dissatisfied"** and **"Neutral"** categories, each with 10 responses. The 14 people who were **dissatisfied** or **very dissatisfied** represent an important group that needs to be analysed in more detail to understand the areas of dissatisfaction.

5.3.2.5 Satisfaction index by locality

Table 14: Breakdown of responses by location and satisfaction index

Satisfaction index	Workforce
Unsatisfactory	10
Abobo	1
Station	1
Bingerville	1
Abbata village	1
Cocody	2
CAMPUS	1
Mermoz	1
Koumassi	1
Sicogi	1
Treichville	2
AVENUE 7	1
Rue 12 Avenue 11 Quartier Apollo	1
Yopougon	3
MILITARY CAMP	1
New district	1
Yopougon	1
Neutral	10
Abobo	1
PK18	1
Adjame	1
220 homes	1
Bingerville	2
Adjin	1
Gbagba	1
Kong	1
Bougou	1
Koumassi	1
Sogefiha	1
Yamoussoukro	1

Kokrenou	1
Yopougon	3
Lokoa	1
Niangon	1
Red roof	1
Satisfactory	13
Abobo	1
Akeikoi	1
Adjame	2
Paillet	1
Williamsville	1
Bingerville	1
Gbagba extension	1
Cocody	3
Akouedo attié	1
Faya	1
Saint Jean	1
Duekoue	2
Ahoussabougou	1
Residential	1
Ferkessedougou	1
Lanviara	1
Mbengue	1
Mbengue	1
Yopougon	2
millionaire	1
Selmer	1
Very unsatisfactory	4
Adjame	1
Index	1
Daloa	1
Olive trees	1
Treichville	1

Km3	1
Yopougon	1
Ananera grove	1
Very satisfactory	2
Yopougon	2
Bel air	1
Sea salt	1
Total	39

Among the 39 respondents, there were two neighbourhoods in the Yopougon commune where respondents said they were very satisfied with safety, namely Bel-air and Sel-mer, and 4 communes where respondents said they were very dissatisfied, namely : Adjame (indénié) Daloa (Les oliviers) Treichville(Km3) Yopougon (Ananeraie)

5.3.2.6 safety

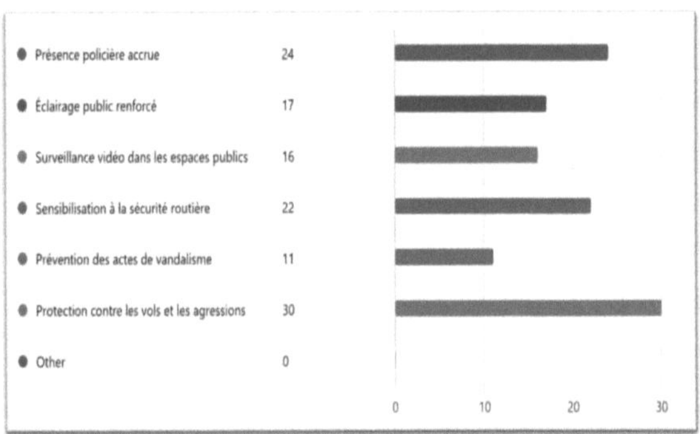

Figure 7: Breakdown of responses by safety area

An analysis of all the responses shows that three areas of security clearly stand out as being the most important for respondents:

Protection against theft and assault: This **is** by far the most frequently cited area, underlining the importance of security for people and their property.

Increased police presence: A stronger, visible police presence is seen as an effective way of deterring crime and intervening quickly in the event of an incident.

Raising awareness of road safety: Road safety is also a major concern, indicating an awareness of the risks associated with traffic and a desire to see concrete actions put in place.

5.3.2.7 Witnesses or victims of crime or security incidents

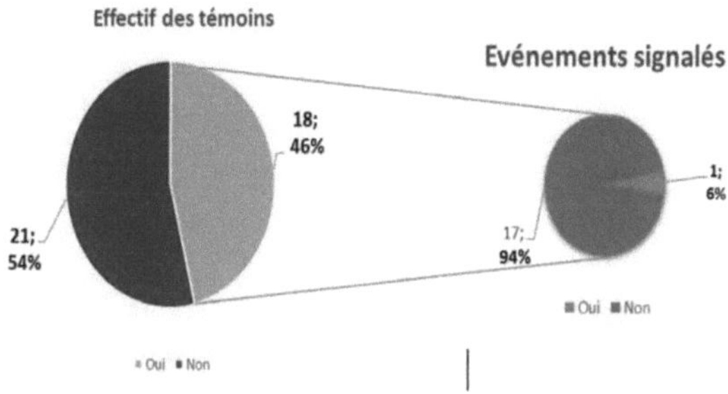

Figure 8: Breakdown of witnesses or victims of crime or security incidents

Of the 39 respondents, 18 said they had witnessed or been the victim of a crime or security incident, and only one of these 18 had reported it to the relevant authorities. Given this low reporting rate, 97% of respondents were in favour of setting up an application that would enable them to report various events. As the following table shows:

Table 15: Participants' opinions

Favourable for a application	Workforce	Percentage
No	1	3%
Yes	38	97%
Grand total	39	100%

5.4 Interpretation of data collected from forms

The data collected enabled us to find out that 8 people, or 18% of respondents, had access to a space where they could consult pass/fail rates. The available spaces used are varied, ranging from physical spaces to electronic spaces (DRENNA, Ecole, Facebook, Google, www.mena.org) but there is no predominance of one type of electronic space.

5.5 Recommendations

After analysing the responses, we can make the following recommendations:

- **Reinforcing anonymity**: Enabling residents to provide information without fear of reprisal.
- **Improving access**: The results show that people do not have sufficient access to the few spaces on offer. It would be beneficial to develop accessible solutions specifically for them.
- **Standardization of spaces**: It could be useful to promote a predominant type of space, such as a centralized website, to facilitate access to information.
- **Increasing the police presence on** the ground, particularly in high-risk areas.
- **Develop video surveillance:** Install surveillance cameras in strategic public spaces.
- **Improve public lighting:** Increase lighting in dark, poorly lit areas.
- **Awareness campaigns:** Raising public awareness of road safety rules and crime prevention.
- **Involving citizens :** Involving citizens in defining and implementing implementation of security policies.
- **Regularly evaluate the policies put in place:** Put in place performance indicators to measure the effectiveness of the actions undertaken.

5.6 Description of the data collection deployment protocol at use of data

5.6.1 Grid each city by neighbourhood

Each city will be divided into several distinct districts to make it easier to manage and organise the data.

5.6.2 Allocate an "administrator" role by theme for certain local residents

Certain residents will be appointed as administrators for each theme (education, safety, health, sports, etc.) to oversee the collection and management of data in their neighbourhood.

5.6.3 Creation of a theme by an administrator

Administrators will be responsible for creating specific themes based on the needs and concerns of their neighbourhood.

5.6.4 Provide the content of the event.

The administrators will provide the input template so that residents can give more details about the events and themes created. However, the protocol for this will depend on the theme.

5.6.4.1 education theme protocol

This section presents the players involved and the protocol for setting up an information form.

5.6.4.1.1 Main actors

Key players in the education theme include :

- **Teachers and head teachers**: Responsible for implementing educational activities and managing pupils.
- **Neighbourhood administrators**: They play a central role in planning, managing resources and overseeing educational initiatives.

5.6.4.1.2 Secondary actors

Supporting actors include :

- **Parents**: Parents are involved in their children's school life and must be kept informed of any initiatives or changes relating to education.
- **The information system** (server): This system is responsible for collecting and storing data relating to educational initiatives, facilitating the analysis of school performance, and enabling communication with educational stakeholders.

5.6.4.1.3 Action protocol for an event on the theme of education

Specific action steps for an event linked to the theme of education :

1. **Reporting an educational need or problem**: Teachers, parents or even pupils may identify a need or problem within the local education system (e.g. lack of books, absence of teachers, problems with the school canteen, etc.). They inform their local education administrator.

2. **Verification by the neighbourhood administrator**: The local education administrator verifies the nature and extent of the need or problem. This stage involves validating the information and assessing the urgency of the intervention.

3. **Coordination with education authorities**: If the problem or need is validated, the administrator contacts the relevant education authorities (Ministry of Education, school board, etc.) to obtain resources or guidelines for resolving the problem.

4. **Creating a communication space**: A dedicated space is created on the digital platform. This space can include a **guided form** so that teachers, parents or students can share their suggestions, concerns or additional information. For example, parents could indicate their children's specific needs in terms of teaching materials.

5. **Data collection and analysis**: The information gathered through the platform (concerns, suggestions for improvement, school results, etc.) is centralised and analysed by the information system (server). This process helps to identify the most frequent problems or the most pressing needs.

6. **Implementing solutions**: After analysing the data, concrete actions are taken. This could include distributing school materials, repairing or improving infrastructure, organising training for teachers, or introducing new teaching methods.

7. **Monitoring and communication with the education community**: Once the measures have been put in place, the administrator and the relevant authorities share the results with parents, teachers and pupils via the digital platform. Meetings or workshops can also be organised to inform the community of progress made or future measures.

This education protocol once again highlights a collaborative approach, where **teachers**, **neighbourhood administrators** and **parents** work together to identify needs and improve learning conditions. The information system plays a key role in facilitating data collection and analysis. By enabling the various stakeholders to voice their concerns and monitor progress, this approach ensures better management of educational resources and promotes community involvement in children's educational success. Centralised and well-communicated information ensures continuous improvement in the quality of education, while guaranteeing transparency in the actions taken.

5.6.4.2 Protocol for the safety theme

This section presents the players involved and the protocol for setting up an information form.

5.6.4.2.1 Main actors

Key players are the persons or entities directly responsible for processing information or managing the event. In this context, the main players may be :

- **Neighbourhood administrators**: They play a central role as a point of contact for residents, responsible for receiving and handling alerts.

- **The competent authorities**: These authorities include the police, school heads, municipal services or any other body empowered to intervene in reported incidents.

- **Residents**: They also play a central role as resource people for our system. They will be responsible for informing the platform.

5.6.4.2.2 Secondary actors

A key secondary player in this process is the **information system** or **server**. This system is responsible for storing and managing the data collected through online forms, making it easier to analyse and share information with stakeholders.

5.6.4.2.3 Action protocol

The process described follows a clear set of steps to effectively manage alerts and incidents reported by residents:

1. **Incident reporting by residents**: Residents of a neighbourhood or locality identify a problem or incident relating to security (for example, a burglary or an act of vandalism). They contact the neighbourhood administrator to report it.
2. **Verification of veracity by the neighbourhood administrator**: Once informed, the neighbourhood administrator verifies the authenticity and seriousness of the information received. This stage is crucial to ensure that only valid situations are passed on to the authorities, so as not to clog up the system with false alerts.

3. **Notification to the appropriate authorities**: If the incident is confirmed, the administrator will forward the details to the relevant authorities (police, fire brigade, etc.) so that immediate action can be taken.

4. **Creating a space on the platform**: The administrator opens a dedicated space on the digital platform where a guided form is made available to residents. This form is used to collect additional information, including details of the incident, witnesses, circumstances and other relevant aspects.

5. **Data collection and analysis**: The data collected through these forms is then processed by the information system (server). An in-depth analysis is carried out to identify trends or recurring problems in the neighbourhood or community.

6. **Communication of results**: After processing, the results and conclusions are shared with the public on the platform, to inform them of the actions taken and future safety measures. This also promotes transparency between administrators, authorities and citizens.

This protocol highlights a collaborative model in which citizens play an active role in managing safety in their community. It is supported by a modern information system that enables data to be centralised and rigorously managed. Thanks to the digital platform, residents can not only report incidents, but also track the responses and actions taken. The process ensures continuous and effective communication between various stakeholders to improve local safety. The themes will be published and made available to all residents via our information system, enabling wide participation.

5.6.5 Right to submit completed form on .

To be able to add comments and participate in the intelligence of the locality, you must be a resident of the city and registered on the platform. It should be noted that comments are intended to be constructive and not to contradict a speaker. Residents are encouraged to comment constructively on topics using online forms, enabling qualitative data to be collected.

5.6.6 Limited lifespan of the theme

The time limit for commenting will be one month, but this can be adjusted by the administrators according to specific needs.

5.6.7 Carry out a statistical analysis of the event for consultation

At the end of the comment period, a statistical analysis will be carried out to summarise the data collected, identify trends and inform future decisions.

5.7 data model

The data model will be established by identifying all the entities required to deploy the solution. The approach is to track each thematic event under consideration, then extract the entities from the collection and exploitation scenario as defined in the protocol. The relational data model will be described in another publication.

5.8 Implementation of the solution

Our architectural choice is a 3-tier architecture, incorporating a web layer, an application layer and a data layer. This architecture enables clear separation of concerns, facilitating maintenance, scalability and system security.

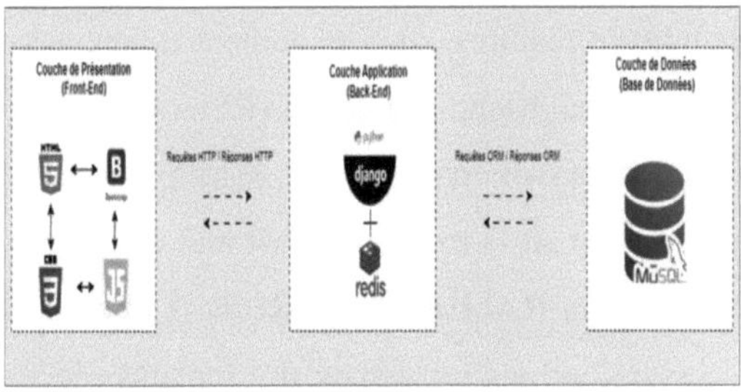

Figure 9: Architectural approach

5.8.1 Web technology Bootstrap html ,

Three main areas

- Create an event layer :

This sub-section enables users to create and manage events. It includes interactive forms and dynamic user interfaces to facilitate the creation of events. This layer is reserved for administrators

- Intelligence layer :

This sub-section is dedicated to collecting and displaying information that is relevant to users. It uses Bootstrap components to present the data in a clear and accessible way.

- Advisory layer

This sub-section offers consultation functionalities, enabling users to search for and consult events and information. It incorporates navigation elements and filters to enhance the user experience.

5.8.2 Application technology (Django and Redis)

For the application layer, we opted for Django and Redis. Django is a Python web framework. It allows us to quickly develop robust and secure applications thanks to its many built-in features, such as authentication, session management and ORM (Object-Relational Mapping). Redis (REmote DIctionary Server) is an in-memory key-value database management system, often used as a cache, database or message broker. It is extremely fast and can store and retrieve data in a few milliseconds using RAM memory. Redis is also capable of persisting data on disk if necessary, although its main use remains processing fast data in memory.

5.8.3 Data technology (MySQL)

The data layer uses MySQL as its database management system. MySQL is a proven choice for web applications because of its performance, reliability and ability to manage large amounts of data. This layer is responsible for storing, retrieving and managing the data needed to run our application.

6 NEXT STAGES

In the next document, we will present the use cases, the sequence diagrams, the data tables and their fields, the implemented forms and an overview of the application.

7 CONCLUSION

In this study, we explored the crucial role of citizen-generated data in improving the quality of services in smart cities. By harnessing these data streams, urban administrations can obtain real-time information on various aspects of urban life, enabling more informed decision-making and proactive responses to community needs. We have detailed the process of collecting, structuring and storing this data, ensuring that it can be interrogated and used effectively. Our collaboration with city administrators and residents to identify key QoS parameters and develop a suitable data model underlines the importance of involving all stakeholders in the data ecosystem. This approach not only improves service delivery but also fosters a more engaged and informed citizenry. Future work will focus on refining the data model, strengthening data security measures and broadening the scope of data sources to include more diverse and dynamic information. Ultimately, this research aims to contribute to the development of smarter, more responsive urban environments that prioritise the wellbeing and needs of their residents.

BIBLIOGRAPHY

AlZoman, H., & Alenazi, M. (2020). Smart City Resilient System (SCRS): A Software-Defined Networking (SDN) Based Approach. International Journal of Advanced Computer Science and Applications (IJACSA), 11(5), 23-30. DOI: 10.14569/IJACSA.2020.0110503.

Bender, B., De Haan, L., & Bennett, C. (1995). The Coevolution of Man and Technology.

Revue des Sciences Humaines, 78(2), 123-145.

Brangier, É. (2002). De l'Ergonomie Cognitive à l'Ergonomie de Conception: Vers une Nouvelle Approche de la Coévolution Homme-Technologie. Ergonomie, 25(3), 200-215.

Brangier, É. (2003). L'Évolution de la Relation Homme-Machine: Vers une Approche Écologique et Évolutionniste. Revue d'Anthropologie, 49(1), 101-119.

De Rosnay, J. (2000). L'Homme Symbiotique: Regards sur le Troisième Millénaire. Paris: Seuil.

Griffith, T. L. (2006). Co-Evolution through the Human-Technology Interface: The Impact of Task, Technology, and Individuals. Washington, DC: American Psychological Association.

Laufs, J., Borrion, H., & Bradford, B. (2020). Security in Smart Cities: A Review of the Literature.

Sustainable Cities and Society, 55, 102023. DOI: 10.1016/j.scs.2020.102023.

Lloret, J., Sendra, S., Parra, L., & Parra, L. (2019). Group-Based Communication Protocol for Wireless Sensor Networks in Smart Cities. IEEE Access, 7, 27360-27373. DOI: 10.1109/ACCESS.2019.2901695.

Mohanty, S. P., Choppali, U., & Kougianos, E. (2016). Everything You Wanted to Know About Smart Cities: The Internet of Things is the Backbone. IEEE Consumer Electronics Magazine, 5(3), 60-70. DOI:

10.1109/MCE.2016.2556879.
Ralko, A., & Kumar, N. (n.d.). Cybersecurity in Smart Cities: Strategies and Challenges. Journal of Urban Technology. DOI: 10.1080/10630732.2020.1840500.
Simondon, G. (1958). Du Mode d'Existence des Objets Techniques. Paris: Aubier.
Stiegler, B. (1989). La Technique et le Temps, Tome 1: La Faute d'Épiméthée. Paris: Galilée.
Tu, C. (2018). Quality of Service and Quality of Experience in Smart Cities. IEEE Communications Magazine, 56(12), 88-95. DOI: 10.1109/MCOM.2018.1800174.
Number of Internet users worldwide by region 2023. (n.d.). Statista. Accessed 20 July 2024, at https://fr.statista.com/statistiques/564020/nombre-d-utilisateurs-d-internet-dans- le-monde-en-par-region/

Printed by Books on Demand GmbH, Norderstedt / Germany